I0568877

THE FOG WAS NEVER YOU

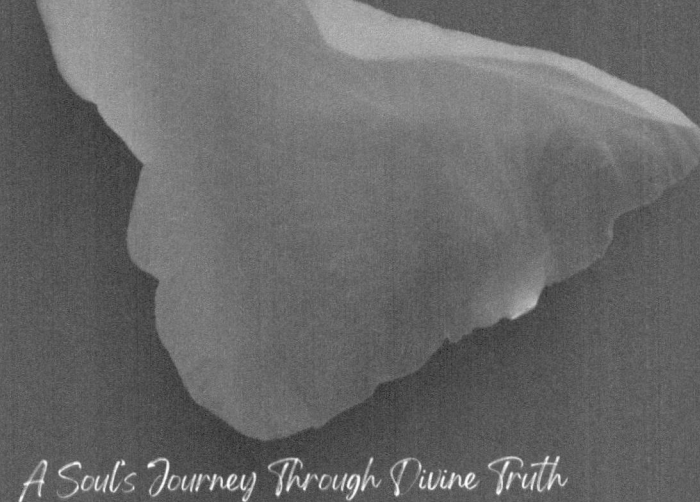

A Soul's Journey Through Divine Truth

the doorway within

Copyright © 2025 The Doorway Within
All rights reserved. No part of this publication
may be copied, stored, or transmitted in any
form or by any means electronic, mechanical,
photocopying, recording, or otherwise
without prior written permission of the
author. This work is a sacred body of truth.
Honor it as you would honor the voice that
guided you here.

Disclaimer

This work is not a substitute for therapy, coaching, religious doctrine, or psychological diagnosis. It does not follow the systems, language, or approaches commonly used by the human self-help or manifesting industry. It exists outside those frameworks intentionally.

This is not healing. This is not transforming. This is not manifesting. This is a return to what was always clear.

The content within is meant to awaken Divine remembrance, not reinforce worldly definitions.

Any decisions made after reading this manual are solely the responsibility of the reader.

TABLE OF CONTENTS

From the Messenger
How to Use This Manual

SECTION TWO: Lies you spiritualized

EN 1 - It wasn't divine timing. It was fear in a holy costume

EN 2 - They told you to evolve. You just learned to perform

EN 3 - You called it surrender. But you were just avoiding truth

EN 4 - You were waiting on a sign. The voice already spoke

EN 5 - It wasn't faith. It was emotional disconnection wearing scripture

EN 6 - You called it being led. But you were just avoiding loss

SECTION THREE: When you thought it was the Divine

EN 1 - It wasn't God. It was guilt dressed like conviction

EN 2 - The Divine never asked you to shrink

EN 3 - You said "God said" but you just didn't want to let go

EN 4 - The Divine didn't delay you. You delayed your own yes

EN 5 - The voice of God doesn't sound like fear

EN 6 - You keep saying it's a test. It's actually a door you won't walk through

SECTION FOUR: Your voice was always the key

EN 1 - You didn't lose yourself. You silenced yourself to survive

EN 2 - You keep asking for clarity. But you already know

EN 3 - Your voice isn't too much. Their comfort is too small

EN 5 - Your discernment isn't broken. You just stopped trusting it

EN 6 - You were never confused. You were trained to doubt

EN 7 - You keep delaying truth so you don't disrupt their peace

<u>SECTION FIVE: The real return</u>

EN 1 - You don't need a new self. You just need to stop abandoning the original

EN 2 - You can't be free while obeying what broke you

EN 3 - You're not called to be liked. You're called to be clear

EN 4 - You already know. Walk in it

EN 6 - Stop speaking it into existence. Obey what already is

EN 7 - Stop asking to be ready. Just move

CLOSING

This isn't the end. It's the exit point

You don't need to heal. You need to remember

Final instruction: Close the book. Live the truth

A Divine Wake-Up

return to what was always clear

From the messenger

I didn't come to teach. I came to tell the
truth. I didn't write this to guide you into
another version of yourself. I didn't come to
convince you that you need more healing,
more evolving, or more shifting.

You've been taught that becoming whole
means chasing what you aren't yet.
But this manual isn't about chasing. It's about
waking up.

Waking up to the lies.
Waking up to the distortions.
Waking up to the places where you called
captivity "faith" and silence "peace."

Humans have sold you an illusion dressed in
self-help.

But this—this is a return.

Not to some better self.
But to the one that never needed fixing
in the first place.

The Divine didn't ask you to perform. Or
hustle. Or explain.

It asked you to remember.
And that's why this book exists.
Read it like a mirror. Not a method.
Let the truth find you where no one else
could. And let it wake you up.

—the messenger

Read This Before Anything Else

This isn't a journal. This isn't a workbook. This isn't something to study. This is a mirror. A disruption. A manual to return you to what was always clear before the noise.

Here's how to use it:
Don't rush. One entry at a time is enough. Let the message land. Don't dissect it. This is not meant to be decoded. Truth is felt, not overanalyzed. Let it confront you. If something stings, that's the place to pause not defend. Read with your spirit, not just your eyes. When you feel the truth, stop. Sit with it. Let it reveal what's been buried.

You won't find steps here. You'll find sentences that remove the blindfold. Take your time. Let it wake you up. Then move different. Because now you know.

Section One:
What You've Outgrown

<u>SECTION ONE: What You've Outgrown</u>

EN 1 - It wasn't growth. It was survival in disguise

EN 2 - You thought you were processing. You were just repeating pain that was never yours

EN 3 - You didn't let go. You just stopped hoping they'd change

EN 4 - You called it loyalty. It was actually fear

EN 5 - You outgrew what you used to pray for

EN 6 - You called it wisdom. It was actually disobedience

EN 7 - You got comfortable in what was meant to be temporary

EN 8 - You Didn't Release It. You Just Buried

<u>Soul Interruption:</u>

You called it growth.
But it was just you learning how to survive
without being questioned.

<u>What no one dared to say:</u>

You didn't change.
You adjusted.
Because that's what kept you accepted.
That's what got you applause.
You kept getting praised for being strong,
but no one saw what it cost to keep holding it
all together.

You smiled when you wanted to disappear.
You stayed quiet when the truth was loud.
You shrunk to stay safe then called it
maturity.
But the Divine never asked you to adapt to
what dishonors your truth.
It asked you to come back to what never
changed:
what you've known, what you've felt, what
you were told to bury. Survival taught you to
behave.

Truth asks you to return.

<u>*Here's your step to break the fear:*</u>

What role have you played just to be
accepted?
Drop it today.
Don't explain it.
Don't soften it.
Just stop performing what was never
real.
Let the discomfort speak. That's where
your clarity lives.

ENTRY 2: You Thought You Were Processing. You Were Just Repeating Pain That Was Never Yours

<u>Soul Interruption:</u>

You didn't need to explain it again.
You needed to stop carrying it like it was yours
to hold.

<u>*What no one dared to say:*</u>

You thought revisiting it would bring peace.
That if you kept talking about it, you'd
eventually feel free.

But you weren't releasing anything.
You were replaying it over and over hoping
someone would finally hear what they
refused to see the first time.

You were never asked to keep proving your
pain.
But because no one held it with you, you
started holding it for everyone.

That wasn't clarity.
It was captivity.

The Divine never demanded a breakdown to
prove you were real. Only humans did.

Here's your step to break the fear:

What story do you keep revisiting not
because it sets you free, but because it
reminds you the pain was real?

You don't owe it another replay.
You don't need to silence it either.
You just need to stop making it your
identity.
Set it down. Walk forward without taking it
with you.

Soul Interruption:

Letting go didn't happen when you found peace.
It happened when you accepted they wouldn't give you what they never had to offer.

What no one dared to say:

You waited for change because you still believed in potential.

You stayed longer because you thought your love would soften their pride.
But what you were really doing was bargaining with their patterns.

Trying to change the outcome by staying the same.
You thought letting go would mean you gave up.
But really, it meant you stopped betraying yourself.
Letting go isn't cold.

It's clear.

It says, "I no longer need to lose myself to love you."

<u>Here's your step to break the fear:</u>

Where are you still hoping their change
will redeem your sacrifice?

That's not love. That's survival.
Walk away from the outcome.
Come back to yourself.

<u>*Soul Interruption:*</u>

Loyalty didn't ask you to shrink.
Fear did. And you obeyed it because it wore
the mask of commitment.

<u>*What no one dared to say:*</u>

You stayed because leaving felt unsafe.
You confused endurance with devotion.
But the Divine never asked you to prove your
worth through suffering.

You weren't loyal.
You were scared to disappoint.
Scared to be alone.
Scared to be misunderstood.
And so you stayed longer than you had peace.
You gave more than you had.
You called it love.
But it was survival wrapped in sacrifice.

Here's your step to break the fear:

What are you still calling loyalty that's really just fear of loss.

Sit with that.
Let honesty name what fear has been hiding.
And let truth walk you out.

<u>*Soul Interruption:*</u>

What once felt like a gift now feels like something you have to manage.

<u>*What no one dared to say:*</u>

It came in a season when you were still learning how to receive.
It felt like the answer.

You were grateful.
But now, it feels off.
Heavier. Restrictive. Small.

But because you once celebrated it, you're afraid to release it.
You think letting go means being ungrateful.
It just means you're finally honest.
The Divine gives freely but never demands you stay bound to something you've outgrown.

<u>*Here's your step to break the fear:*</u>

What are you still holding onto because
you once labeled it "the blessing"
You don't need to disrespect it just stop
calling it home.

Move forward. The way has already been
cleared.

<u>Soul Interruption:</u>

You weren't being wise.
You were playing safe and calling it obedience.

<u>What no one dared to say:</u>

You paused, and called it patience.
You held back, and called it discernment.
But wisdom isn't stillness rooted in fear.

It doesn't stall.
It doesn't wait for comfort.
It doesn't need confirmation five more times.
You already heard the instruction.
You already knew the answer.

But you didn't want to obey because obedience meant loss.

So you chose the delay and named it wisdom.
But delay is still disobedience when you already know. The Divine doesn't speak in circles.
Only fear does.

Here's your step to break the fear:

What have you been calling "wise" that's really you avoiding the move.

You're not confused.
You're just scared.
Move with truth not delay dressed as logic.

Soul Interruption:

Just because it didn't hurt anymore
didn't mean it was meant to stay.

What no one dared to say:

You didn't settle because it was
right.
You settled because it was familiar.
It stopped hurting, so you stopped
questioning.
But comfort isn't confirmation.

It's just the absence of friction and
sometimes, you confused that for
peace.
You stayed because it made sense.
Because starting over felt heavy.
Because convincing yourself it was
"good enough" was easier than
facing the truth that it expired. But
the Divine didn't send you to build
altars in places meant to be crossed
through.

**You didn't miss your season you
overstayed it.**

Name what you know has expired.
Stop calling it stable just because it
no longer shakes you.

You're not stuck you're stalling in a
room you were never meant to
decorate. Open the door.

Walk out without apologizing.

ENTRY 8: You Didn't Release It. You Just Buried It

Soul Interruption:

You didn't let it pass through.
You just silenced it and called that strength.

What no one dared to say:

You didn't face it.
You covered it.
Under performance.
Under responsibility.
Under pretending you were okay.
You stopped speaking on it so you
convinced yourself it was over.
But buried truth doesn't disappear.
It lingers.

It leaks into how you show up.
How you protect yourself.
How you keep distance.
The Divine never asked you to carry it in
silence. It asked you to name it so it
would lose its grip. This wasn't about
fixing.
It was about honesty.
And you've been avoiding it long enough.

Here's your step to break the fear:

What are you still covering with
"I'm fine"
Say it for real this time.
Let the silence break.
Let the weight drop.

Section Two
Lies You
Spiritualized

SECTION TWO: Lies you spiritualized

EN 1 - It wasn't divine timing. It was fear in a holy costume

EN 2 - They told you to evolve. You just learned to perform

EN 3 - You called it surrender. But you were just avoiding truth

EN 4 - You were waiting on a sign. The voice already spoke

EN 5 - It wasn't faith. It was emotional disconnection wearing scripture

EN 6 - You called it being led. But you were just avoiding loss

ENTRY 1: It Wasn't Divine Timing. It Was Fear in a Holy Costume

Soul Interruption:

You said you were waiting on the right time.
But the truth is... you were scared.

What no one dared to say:

Fear taught you to call delay
"discernment."
Avoidance taught you to name hesitation
"God's will."

But timing wasn't the issue. Obedience
was.
The voice already spoke.
You just didn't like what it asked you to
walk away from.

So you waited. And while you waited, fear
wrapped itself in scripture, in rituals, in
routines and made you think you were
being wise.

But the Divine doesn't manipulate with
fear.
And silence isn't always sacred.
Sometimes it's just avoidance with a halo
on.
You weren't being still.
You were stalling.

What you called "timing" was actually fear.

Now think what it's been costing you.
Obey the first instruction.
The voice never changed.

Soul Interruption:

You didn't evolve.
You just adjusted to environments that
punished your truth.

What no one dared to say:

They called it growth.
But it was really pressure to stay
likable.
So you reshaped yourself not to be
better,
but to be accepted.

You kept quiet when the truth felt loud.
You smiled when you were tired of
performing.
You made yourself smaller so others
wouldn't feel exposed.

But that wasn't growth.
That was survival.

That was the performance they
applauded
because it protected their comfort.
The Divine never asked you to play a
role.
It asked you to remember who you
were before you adjusted to be
digestible.

Here's your step to break the fear:

Where are you still pretending just
to keep the peace?

Let the performance end.
Say the thing you've been holding
back and let their discomfort reveal
what was never yours to carry.

ENTRY 3: You called it surrender. But you were just avoiding truth

<u>Soul Interruption:</u>

You didn't surrender.
You turned away from what truth asked you to face.

<u>What no one dared to say:</u>

You called it surrender, but really you were tired of deciding. Tired of the pressure to get it right.

So you let go.
Not to obey but to escape the truth you didn't want to admit. You said "let it flow" when the Divine already gave direction.

You sat still and spiritualized your silence,
but the truth was loud the whole time.
This wasn't peace.
It was passivity.

The Divine doesn't ask you to disappear.
It asks you to walk in what's already clear.
You weren't surrendering.
You were avoiding the cost of honesty.

Here's your step to break the fear:

What are you still covering with "I'm fine"
Say it for real this time.
Let the silence break. Let the weight drop.

ENTRY 4: You were waiting on a sign.
The voice already spoke

<u>Soul Interruption:</u>

You didn't need more clarity. You needed more
courage to move on what you already knew.

<u>What no one dared to say:</u>

You didn't face it.
You covered it.
Under performance.
Under responsibility.
Under pretending you were okay.
You stopped speaking on it so you
convinced yourself it was over.
But buried truth doesn't disappear.
It lingers.

It leaks into how you show up.
How you protect yourself.
How you keep distance.
The Divine never asked you to carry it in
silence. It asked you to name it so it
would lose its grip. This wasn't about
fixing.
It was about honesty.
And you've been avoiding it long
enough.

Here's your step to break the fear:

What are you still covering with
"I'm fine"
Say it for real this time.
Let the silence break.
Let the weight drop.

<u>Soul Interruption:</u>

You didn't trust the Divine.
You just numbed yourself and called it belief.

<u>*What no one dared to say:*</u>

You weren't standing in faith.
You were detaching from reality
and covering it in spiritual language.
You said "I trust God" while refusing
to feel the disappointment.
You quoted verses to silence emotions
you didn't want to deal with.

That wasn't trust.
It was shutdown.
It was emotional escape wrapped in
religious habit.

The Divine never asked you to hide
your humanity. It asked you to bring
it raw, real, and unfiltered. Faith
doesn't disconnect you from what's
real. It gives you the courage to walk
through it.

Here's your step to break the fear:

What emotion have you been covering
with "faith language"?

Say it plainly.
Feel it honestly.
Let truth and God meet you there.

<u>Soul Interruption:</u>

It wasn't discernment.
It was fear dressed up like direction.

<u>What no one dared to say:</u>

You said "I feel led to stay."
But really you were afraid of what
walking away would cost you. You
weren't being led. You were circling a
decision because letting go felt like
failure.

So you spiritualized the delay.
You waited for clarity when the truth had
already revealed itself.

This isn't about Divine guidance.
This is about your fear of loss, of
disappointment, of no longer being
needed, chosen, or understood.

But the Divine doesn't keep you stuck in
the name of being led.

It calls you to move even when movement
feels like grief.

Here's your step to break the fear:

What have you been holding onto
because you're afraid of what leaving it
will say about you?

Call it what it is.
Not led.
Not stuck.

Just unwilling to lose what was never
meant to stay.

Section Three: When you thought it was the Divine

SECTION THREE: When you thought it was the Divine

EN 1 - It wasn't God. It was guilt dressed like conviction

EN 2 - The Divine never asked you to shrink

EN 3 - You called it surrender. But you were just avoiding truth

EN 4 - You said "God said" but you just didn't want to let go

EN 5 - The voice of God doesn't sound like fear

EN 6 - You called it being led. But you were just avoiding loss

Soul Interruption:
What you called obedience
was actually fear trying to earn forgiveness.

What no one dared to say:
You didn't stay because the Divine told
you to. You stayed because guilt
convinced you it was the holy thing to
do.

They made you believe that being
faithful meant enduring what
dishonored your soul.
So you tolerated it. You kept going.
You let guilt lead you into silence, self-
abandonment, and spiritual confusion.

You felt heavy, not holy.
But you convinced yourself it was God.
The Divine doesn't speak in shame.
It doesn't hold you hostage.
It doesn't twist your spirit to make you
obedient.

What you followed wasn't conviction.
It was guilt dressed in religious
language.
And it kept you bound.

Here's your step to break the fear:

Name where guilt still holds authority in your life. If it made you feel small, it wasn't sacred.

Step out of it. Truth won't keep you trapped.

Soul Interruption:

You made yourself small to be accepted.
But the Divine never needed you to be less in order to be worthy or loved.

What no one dared to say:

You weren't quiet because it felt holy.
You were quiet because being seen too clearly scared you.

You called it humility.
You called it wisdom.
But it was fear.
Fear of being called too much.
Fear of being rejected for your clarity.
Fear of what would happen if you took up space without apology.

And so you shrunk.
You made your light easier to look at.
You adjusted your truth to fit into rooms that never had the capacity for you.
But the Divine never asked for your silence.
It never asked you to dim what was sacred.
It asked you to show up fully. Not louder. Just no longer hidden.

Here's your step to break the fear:

Call out the space where you still shrink
to be tolerated.

Then walk in fully.
No apology.
No translation.
Just truth.

<u>*Soul Interruption:*</u>
You weren't being obedient.
You were stalling behind spiritual words because the truth hurt too much to face.

<u>*What no one dared to say:*</u>

You said "God told me to stay."
But deep down, you knew you were just afraid to leave.

You dressed the delay in spiritual language.
You called it confirmation.
You called it loyalty. But it was fear.
You couldn't admit it had expired so you used God's name to make it easier to tolerate.

But the Divine doesn't need to be used as a cover for what you already know you're afraid to release. Truth doesn't need a loophole.
It just needs your honesty.

Obedience is walking away before anyone else understands why. The instruction wasn't for them. It was for you.

<u>*Here's your step to break the fear:*</u>

What are you still covering with "I'm
fine"
Say it for real this time.
Let the silence break.
Let the weight drop.

Soul Interruption:

You weren't waiting on timing.
You were afraid to say yes to what truth
demanded.

What no one dared to say:

You blamed the delay on the Divine.
But it was you.
You stalled.
You asked for signs. You sat in circles of
"not yet" and "still praying."
But the truth was already clear. And you
didn't want to move.

Not because it wasn't time but because
obedience would cost you control,
comfort, or connection.

So you called it waiting.
You said "Divine timing." But that was a
cover. It was fear - fear of what truth
would disrupt.

Fear of what you'd have to leave behind.
Fear of what you'd have to face if you
finally said yes. But the Divine wasn't
holding anything back. You were.

<u>*Here's your step to break the fear:*</u>

What have you been avoiding by calling
it "waiting"?

Say yes now without overthinking, over
explaining, or asking for another sign.
The truth already spoke.
Follow it.

Soul Interruption:

If it sounds like punishment, it's not God. If it
made you shrink, it wasn't God. If it made you
panic, it wasn't truth. It's fear pretending to be
guidance.

What no one dared to say:

You followed voices that unsettled you
and called it wisdom.
You stayed in places that silenced you
and called it obedience.
You were told fear was divine direction.

But it wasn't.
It was confusion dressed up in sacred
words.
And it trained you to chase anxiety
instead of trusting what was already
clear.

The Divine never speaks in threat.
Never moves through panic.
Never pulls you into worry and calls it
guidance.

You weren't confused.
You were following a voice that never
came from God.

Here's your step to break the fear:

Where have you let fear act like it had the final say? Silence it.

The real voice already spoke. And it never needed fear to be heard.

<u>Soul Interruption:</u>

You don't need to pass a test.
You just need to stop circling the truth.

<u>*What no one dared to say:*</u>

You've called it a test because that's
easier than calling it a choice.
You keep asking for strength.
But the step has always been right in
front of you. This isn't a test. It's a door.

And you've been standing in front of it,
praying, overthinking, waiting for peace
when peace already came packaged in
truth.
You were never being tested. You were
being told. And you didn't want to move
unless it felt safe. But the Divine doesn't
need to prove anything to you. It gave
you direction.

You either walk through the door
or stay where you were never meant to
settle.

Here's your step to break the fear:

Stop naming it a test.
Call it what it is: instruction.
Then follow it. You already know where
it leads.

Section Four: Your voice was always the key

SECTION FOUR: Your voice was always the key

EN 1 - You didn't lose yourself. You silenced yourself to survive

EN 2 - You keep asking for clarity. But you already know

EN 3 - Your voice isn't too much. Their comfort is too small

EN 5 - Your discernment isn't broken. You just stopped trusting it

EN 6 - You were never confused. You were trained to doubt

EN 7 - You keep delaying truth so you don't disrupt their peace

ENTRY 1: You Didn't Lose Yourself. You Silenced Yourself to Survive

<u>*Soul Interruption:*</u>

You didn't disappear.
You were just quiet in rooms that didn't know how to hold your truth.

<u>*What no one dared to say:*</u>

You weren't confused.
You were careful.
You watched what you said.
You adjusted how you moved.
You edited your truth to fit inside what others were comfortable with.
And slowly you started fading into roles you never agreed to.

You never lost yourself.
You buried parts of you to stay accepted.
And now, what feels like emptiness is just the sound of your voice waiting to return.
God never told you to hide.
That was survival. And survival is over.

Here's your step to break the fear:

Where are you still whispering when you're supposed to speak? Stop softening the truth.

The voice within you isn't lost it's just been waiting for your permission to come back.

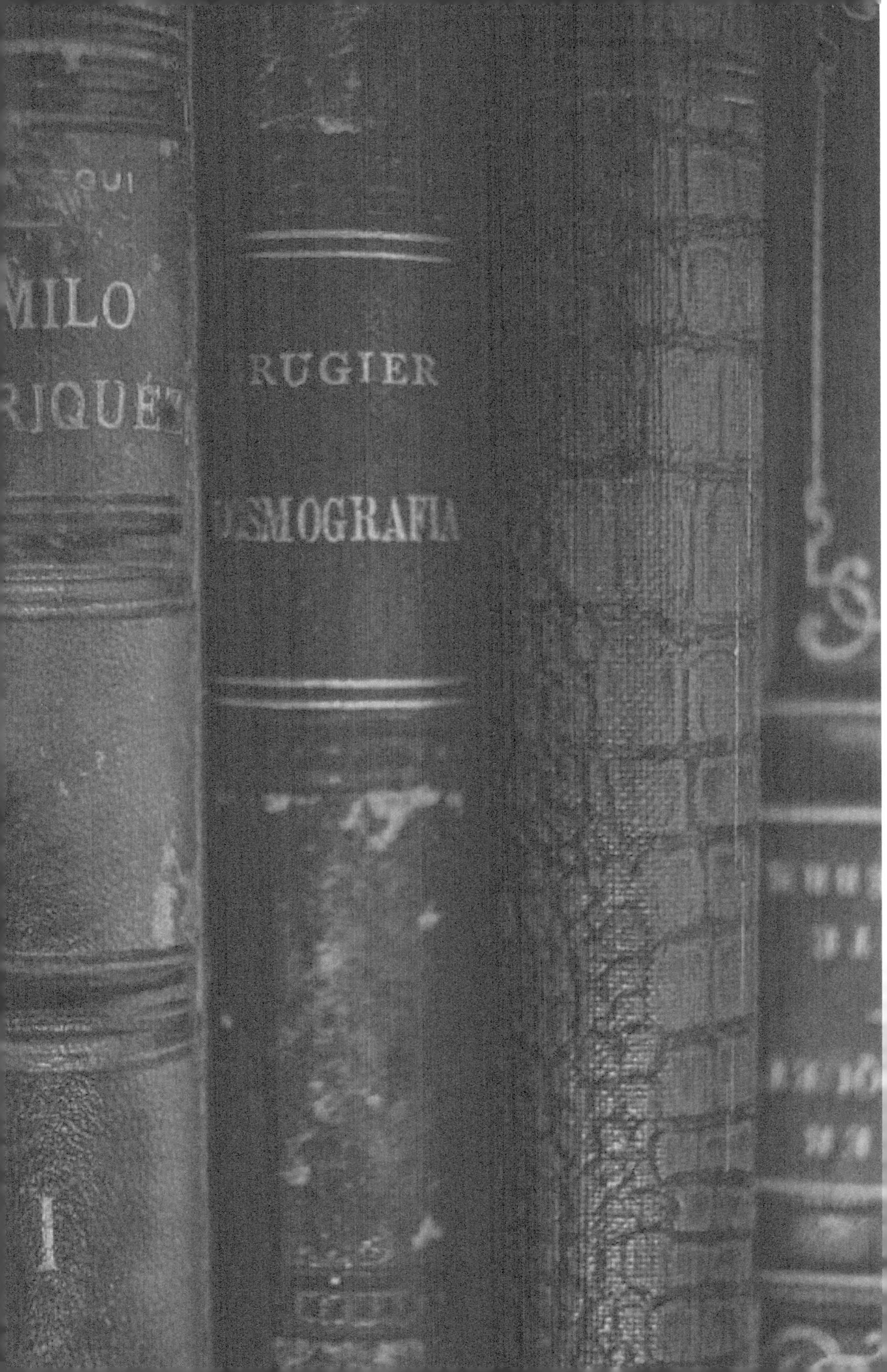
MILO
RUGIER
SMOGRAFIA
I

<u>Soul Interruption:</u>

You're not confused.
You're just avoiding the cost of obeying what you already heard.

<u>What no one dared to say:</u>

You've been calling it unclear but it's always been loud. You're not lacking direction.
You're avoiding what direction requires.
You wanted the next step without having to release the last one.
You prayed for peace, but peace only lives where truth is followed.

The Divine didn't go silent. You did.

And the longer you pretend not to know,
the longer you stay disconnected from your own authority.
You're not waiting for confirmation.
You're waiting for comfort.
And truth doesn't always come with comfort
it comes with clarity.

Here's your step to break the fear:

You already know.
Stop pretending you don't. Walk in it
without flinching.

Soul Interruption:

You've been shrinking so others wouldn't feel stretched. But that's not humility. That's fear.

What no one dared to say:

You adjusted your tone.
You made your truth easier to swallow.
You chose silence over confrontation
and called it wisdom. But let's be honest
you weren't protecting peace.

You were protecting comfort.
Theirs. And every time you swallowed
what needed to be said, you told your
voice it was too loud to be loved.

But God didn't give you a quiet message.
God gave you a clear one.
And you've been trying to edit it to make
others feel safe. That was never your
job.
If your truth rattles their peace it was
never peace to begin with. Stop making
yourself responsible for how they
receive what was never theirs to carry.

Here's your step to break the fear:

Where are you still editing truth to protect someone's comfort? Say the full sentence.

Let it land without softening it. Your voice was never too much it just didn't fit inside their limits.

Soul Interruption:

You didn't lose your ability to know.
You just stopped believing what you sensed
the first time.

What no one dared to say:

You felt it.
The tension in the room.
The weight behind their words.
The silence that didn't feel safe.
But instead of trusting what you picked
up,
you questioned yourself.

You gave them the benefit of the doubt,
and put your own knowing on mute Not
because you were unsure but because
you were trained to second-guess the
voice inside of you.

You don't need to "learn how to discern."
You already do. You just stopped
listening.
Your spirit doesn't lie.
It's not dramatic.
It's not overreacting.
It's accurate.
But it can't lead you if you keep silencing
it.

Where did you know the truth but stayed
quiet so no one else would feel
uncomfortable?

Say it now.

The voice inside you wasn't wrong. It
was waiting to be trusted again.

<u>Soul Interruption:</u>

Confusion wasn't your natural state.
It was something you were taught.

<u>What no one dared to say:</u>

You didn't second-guess yourself
because you were unsure. You second
guessed yourself because others made
your knowing feel like rebellion They
told you you were overthinking,
overreacting, too sensitive.

So you shrunk your insight and labeled
your clarity as "uncertainty." You were
never confused. You just learned to filter
your truth through everyone else's
comfort. And over time, doubt became
the habit not because it belonged to you,
but because it was handed to you.

God didn't place confusion in you.
People did. And you don't need their
permission to return to what you knew
the first time.

Here's your step to break the fear:

What truth did you tuck away because someone told you it was "too much"? Bring it back.

Say it. Stand in it.

Let doubt lose the access it was never supposed to have.

Soul Interruption:

It's not peace if it costs your voice.
That's control disguised as harmony.

What no one dared to say:

You knew what needed to be said but you paused. Not because you were unclear. But because you didn't want to rattle their comfort. You've delayed truth not for timing,
not for wisdom but because silence was safer than confrontation.

You weren't protecting peace.
You were protecting the illusion of it.
And the longer you wait, the more you keep building a life around what's unspoken.

The Divine didn't place truth in you to be buried. It wasn't meant to be filtered through who can or can't handle it. It was meant to be revealed fully.

Here's your step to break the fear:

What have you been holding back to
keep others at ease?

Say it.

You weren't sent to protect their
comfort.
You were sent to walk in truth.

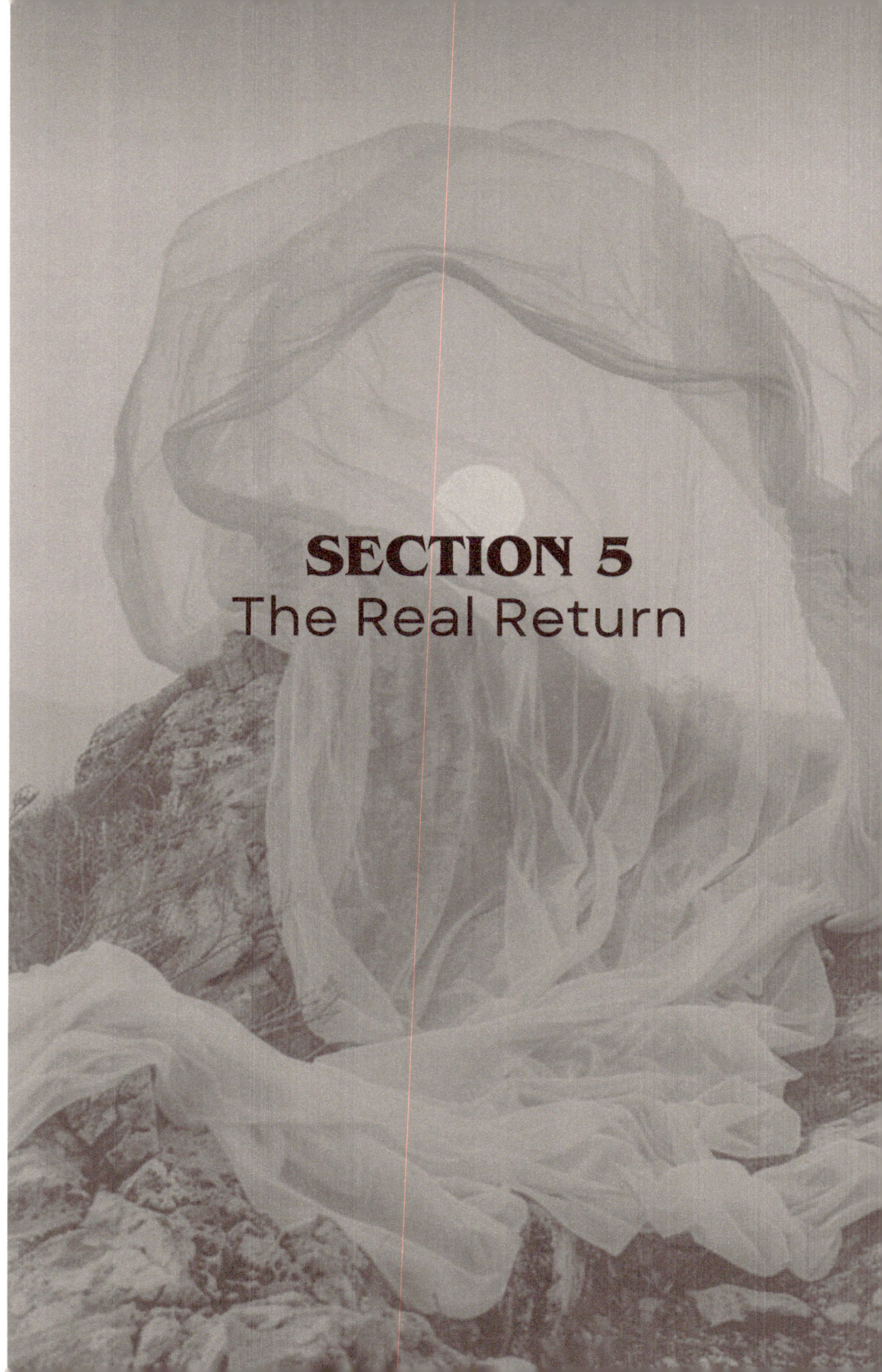

SECTION 5
The Real Return

SECTION FIVE: The real return

EN 1 - You don't need a new self. You just need to stop abandoning the original

EN 2 - You can't be free while obeying what broke you

EN 3 - You're not called to be liked. You're called to be clear

EN 4 - You already know. Walk in it

EN 5 - Your discernment isn't broken. You just stopped trusting it

EN 6 - Stop speaking it into existence. Obey what already is

EN 7 - Stop asking to be ready. Just move

Soul Interruption:

This isn't about becoming someone new.
It's about returning to who you were before
the noise.

What no one dared to say:

You weren't broken.
You were buried.
Under expectations, roles, and survival
habits that taught you being real was
dangerous.
But the original version of you the one
God formed, not the one the world
shaped never left.

You just stopped recognizing her
because performance became easier
than truth.
This isn't about building a better you.

This is about no longer apologizing for
the one that already exists.
God doesn't start over with you.
God brings you back to what's never
changed.

Here's your step to break the fear:

What part of you have you been hiding
to stay accepted?
Bring that self back without permission,
without apology.

That's the real return.

Soul Interruption:

Freedom doesn't live in obedience to dysfunction.
You can't carry truth and bondage in the same breath.

What no one dared to say:

You've been trying to live whole while still submitting to what wounded you.
You call it love. You call it respect. You call it loyalty. But it's not.

It's fear in disguise.
It's the fear of being cast out for walking in clarity.

But God never asked you to obey what keeps you bound.
You weren't called to blend in.
You were called to break the pattern.

<u>*Here's your step to break the fear:*</u>

Name the place where obedience became bondage. You don't owe it another yes.

Freedom won't land in a place where you keep bowing to what you've already outgrown.

Soul Interruption:

Clarity will cost you comfort.
But comfort was never the assignment.

What no one dared to say:

You've been diluting what you carry
because you're afraid of being
misunderstood.
So you settle for being agreeable instead
of being clear. But clarity isn't rude.
Clarity is holy.

And God didn't place truth in you to be
edited. If your clarity makes them
uncomfortable, they were never
connected with the message anyway.

You were never sent to be liked.
You were sent to be accurate.

Here's your step to break the fear:

Where are you still softening your truth
to avoid their reactions? Say it.

Not louder just without hiding.
Your clarity is your assignment.

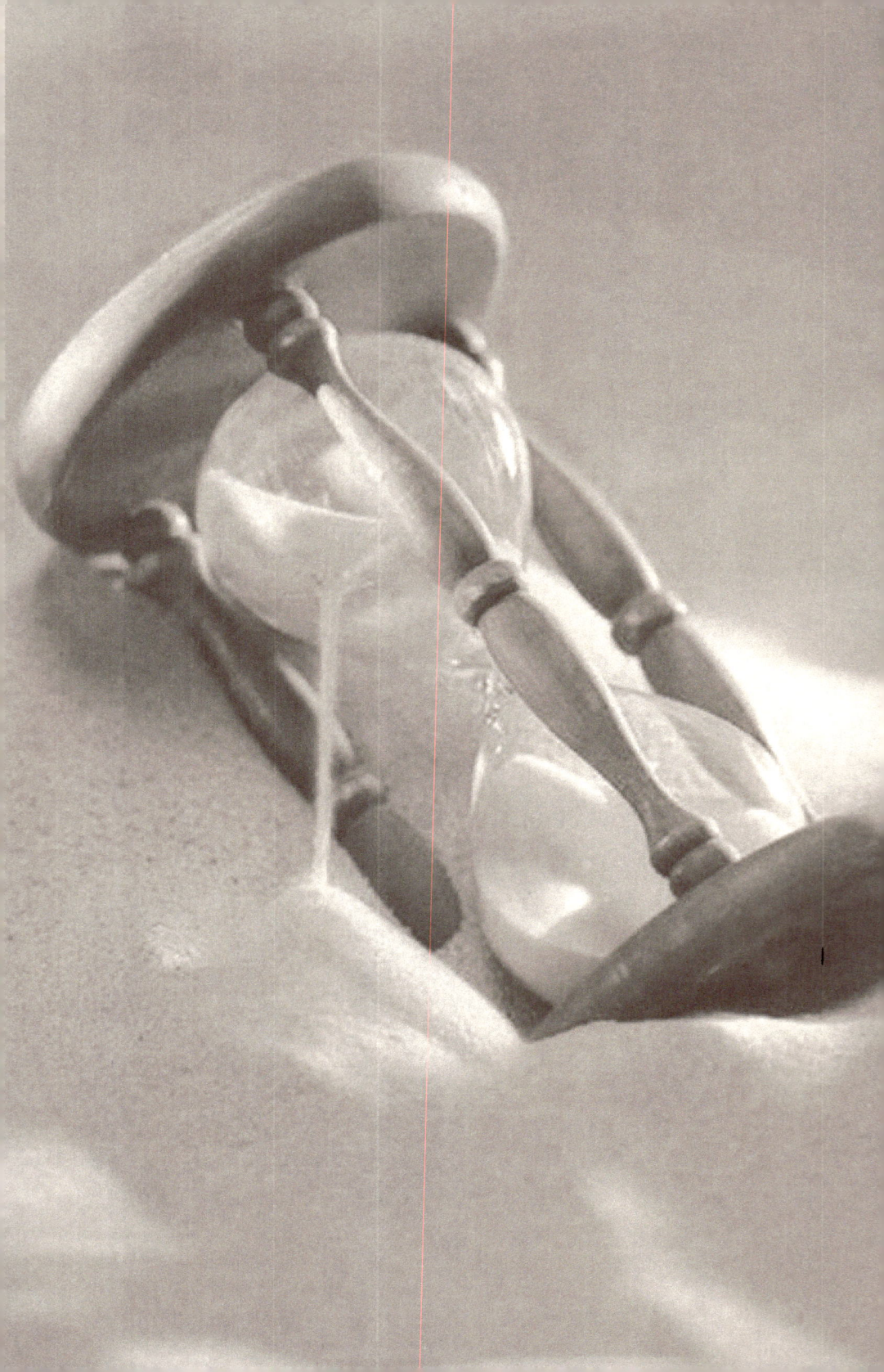

Soul Interruption:

Truth doesn't need more time.
It needs movement.

What no one dared to say:

You've been holding on, asking for signs
and signals but the instruction was
already clear.

You weren't confused.
You were avoiding what obedience would
cost.
You weren't uncertain.
You just didn't want to be
misunderstood.

That quiet knowing inside you. It was
never yours to question. It was God
speaking.

You don't need more time.
You need to stop pretending you don't
already know.

Here's your step to break the fear:

Call it what it is.
Truth doesn't need waiting.
It needs your yes.

Soul Interruption:

That feeling you had? It wasn't a guess.
It was discernment. You didn't lose it you just
stopped believing it was real.

What no one dared to say:

They called it overthinking, but it was
always clarity.
They told you to get confirmation, but
you already had the knowing.
You learned to second-guess what was
already certain because your certainty
made other people uncomfortable.

And so, you silenced what God already
confirmed in you. Discernment doesn't
need validation. It only needs obedience.
And you didn't stop hearing it just got
buried under voices that didn't carry
truth.

God never needed you to explain your
knowing.

The Divine only asked you to follow it.

Here's your step to break the fear:

Stop calling it confusion.
Call it what it is: divine clarity.

Let every time you doubted your
discernment be the reminder of how
deeply you already knew.

Now trust it again.

Soul Interruption:

There was never anything unclear about you. They just didn't want you to remember.

What no one dared to say:

You weren't lost. You were told your clarity was a problem. Taught to shrink it. To delay it. To explain it. But you knew.

Before the noise. Before the guilt. Before the pressure to "make sense." You knew. But the moment you obeyed what didn't sit right.

You disconnected from what never stopped being true.

It wasn't confusion. It was interference. They needed your knowing to look like rebellion. But what God gave you never required permission.

Here's your step to break the fear:

What did you know before anyone
interrupted it?

That's your truth.
Return to it. Speak from there.

<u>*Soul Interruption:*</u>

Silence has never protected you.
It only protected the lie.

<u>*What no one dared to say:*</u>

You keep adjusting your voice so others don't call it "too much." You keep softening the message so they don't feel convicted.
You call it "wisdom."

But it's really delay. You're afraid of being misunderstood, because every time you told the truth, they called it trouble.
You weren't disrupting peace.
You were disturbing comfort that never came from God.

Truth isn't aggressive. It's just direct. And when you speak from what the Divine gave you.

You're not a problem.
You're the proof.

Here's your step to break the fear:

Say what's been burning in your spirit.
And stop checking if they're ready to
hear it.

CLOSING

<u>Soul Interruption:</u>

You didn't need another breakthrough.
You needed a return.
Not to something new but to what was always
clear.
You were never waiting on more power.
You were never broken.
You were just surrounded by voices that
wanted you to forget the one inside.

This wasn't a healing.
This was a revealing.
This wasn't a transformation.
This was a re-entry.
This wasn't a lesson.
This was a Divine interruption.

Final Instruction:

Close the book. Live the truth.

That's it. There is no next step. There is no method.

There is only the voice God already placed in you and it's not asking for permission anymore.

Walk in it.

Final Note from the Messenger

It doesn't matter what religion you follow.
Before the beginning of time, God wanted all
humans to live in peace, love, and harmony.
Not fear. Not shame. Not confusion dressed as
devotion.

I didn't write this for the masses. I wrote it for
the one who remembers.

The one who's done performing. The one who's
tired of being talked down to. The one who
always knew there was more and now refuses to
keep pretending otherwise.

I wrote this because I know what it feels like to
feel empty when all you want are answers.
I know what it means to sit in silence asking,

*Why does this feel so heavy when all
I've done is try to survive?*
And now you will.

I've lived it.
As a Muslim woman,
Navigating a marriage that broke me,
Walking through divorce,
Raising children as a single mother,
Stepping into rooms I was never invited into,
Climbing ladders I was never meant to fit into
all while wondering where God was in the
chaos.
And this is what I now know:
A loving God never punishes.

The chaos was not Divine. It was created by
human hands, built on control, shame, fear,
and lies.
This manual won't tell you what to become.
It will remind you what was always there.

No journaling. No waiting. No step-by-step.
Just truth. And the return to it. You were never
meant to follow.

*You were meant to walk with what
was already placed inside of you.*

The Messenger

www.ingramcontent.com/pod-product-compliance
Lightning Source LLC
Chambersburg PA
CBHW031428120626
46545CB00006B/2317